FESTIVAL

Get your Christmas party started!

GW00493895

This annual belongs to: _____

Age: _____ years old

Class: _____

School: _____

Editor:	Donna Garvin
Design:	Annick Doza
Artwork:	Tim Hutchinson, Arcturus Publishing Limited
Cover Illustration:	Élisabeth Eudes-Pascal (GCI)
Cover Design:	Annick Doza
Photos:	Fleishman Europe (BT Young Scientist and Technology Exhibition)
Stories:	Donna Garvin
ISBN:	978-1-909376-89-2

© 2013 Educate.ie
Tralee Road,
Castleisland,
Co. Kerry,
Ireland
www.educate.ie

The author and publisher have made every effort to trace all copyright holders, but if some have been inadvertently overlooked we would be happy to make the necessary arrangements at the first opportunity.

Contents

4   Pop Scramble Crossword
5   Colour by Numbers (as Gaeilge)
6   Snowy Wordsearch
7   Draw a Penguin (as Gaeilge)
8   Sudoku (as Gaeilge)
9   Quiz Master
10 Feature: Young Scientists in Ireland
12 Spot the Differences (as Gaeilge)
13 Brain Teasers
14 Cone Sequence!
15 Creature Crossword
16 Spot the Differences (as Gaeilge)
17 Feature: Science Facts
18 Pretty Poinsettias
19 Feature: Freaky Critters
20 Top Trees
21 Odd One Out (as Gaeilge)
22 Recipe: Plum Cake
23 Recipe: Chocolate Treats
24 Present Puzzle
25 Snowy Crossword
26 Fun Snowflakes
27 Spot the Differences (as Gaeilge)
28 Quiz Master
29 Story: The Tale of Good King Wenceslas
32 Sweetie Jumble
33 Food Fooler
34 Spot the Differences (as Gaeilge)
35 Matching Cards; Colourful Candles

36 Get Down
38 Picture Puzzler
39 Picture Puzzler
40 Picture Puzzler
41 Picture Puzzler
42 Hidden Pictures™ (as Gaeilge)
44 Spot the Differences (as Gaeilge)
46 Time to Rhyme
48 Art Qs
50 Penguin Path
51 The Hole Story
52 Fun House Maze (as Gaeilge)
54 Picture Puzzler
55 Dog Days
56 Hilarious!
58 Rain Forest Qs
60 Picture Puzzler
61 Raise the Flag
62 Monkey Business
64 Picture Puzzler
65 Be Seated
66 What's Wrong?™ (as Gaeilge)
68 Reptile Qs
70 Picture Puzzler
71 Map Mix-Up
72 Ready, Set, Grow!
74 What's Wrong?™ (as Gaeilge)
76 Answers

Pop Scramble Crossword

Unscramble the pop artists and fill in the grid.

Across

2. SHUER
3. NBECYOE
4. NPIK
6. AFDT NKPU
7. IPULTBL
8. DLAY GAAG
13. NOE CTREIONDI
15. NOBRU SMAR
17. MIDE VALOTO
18. LILW.MA.I
19. CKNII NAMIJ

Down

1. STJUIN IERKTEMBLA
5. LOTAYR WSITF
9. SESJEI J
10. LESENA MEGOZ
11. KOAN
12. ODCY SPSIONM
14. ANIRHNA
16. ERBAUA
20. DEALE

Answers on page 76

Dathaigh le hUimhreacha

Lean an treoir leis an bpictiúr a dhathú.

① dearg　② gorm　③ buí　④ glas
⑤ corcra　⑥ donn　⑦ oráiste　⑧ bándearg

Snowy Wordsearch

Look for these words in the snowball grid. Guess what?
If you put the word 'snow' before each one, they all make new words!

```
            X M B
        M S V R A X S
      A N T S O L X H U
    N Q F X H T L E W R I
  D E A T U G S X D R I F T
  X L A X A U T O D M E D F
C L I P S T O X R Q R J S D L
A V B H W J L A K D C O N E F
B O O T S A P V R G U E P X I
O M X X O X A P O I K E R R
T E N E Z O H G A P A V H
  X L N B H O P A I L J
    M H J K L C B Q F
      S E O H S R T
          G H J
```

STORM	DRIFT	FLAKE	MAN
BOARD	MOBILE	CONE	BALL
SHOES	BOOTS	PLOUGH	SUIT
FALL	CAP	DROP	LEOPARD

Tarraing Piongain

Cóipeáil an pictiúr den phiongain sa ghreille thíos.

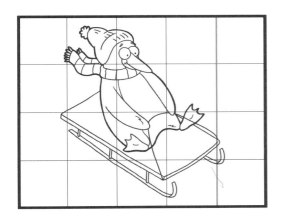

What's the first thing I learned at school?

The elfabet!

Sudoku

		1						9
8	2					6	4	
7	6		4	2		3		
		7	9		6			
	5			4			1	
			2		1	7		
	3			9	5		6	4
	7	4					9	5
9						2		

Críochnaigh na sudoku seo.

Ní mór go mbeadh 45 mar fhreagra ar shuimiú na n-uimhreacha i ngach sraith agus colún.

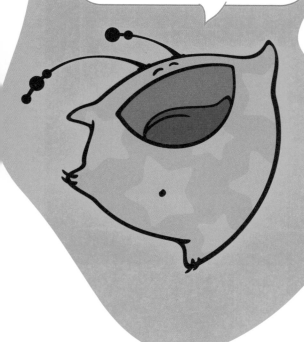

		8					1	
5			8			4		
			6		1	8		
6	4	3	5				2	9
	8			2				3
	9	2			3	1	5	6
		1	7		9			
		6				4		9
		3				6		

Freagraí ar leathanach 76

Quiz Master

1. Who led a gang of outlaws in Sherwood Forest?

2. What was the name of the wizard in the court of King Arthur?

3. Which famous nurse was called the 'Lady with the Lamp'?

4. 'Ping-pong' is another name for which sport?

5. In which country in ancient times was mummification carried out?

6. What is the name of the lion in *The Lion, The Witch and the Wardrobe*?

7. From what country does Lego come?

8. Which ocean liner sank on its maiden voyage in 1912?

9. Wolverine is the leader of which group of superheroes?

10. Crawl, backstroke and butterfly belong to which sport?

11. Rooster, Kerr's pink and golden wonder are varieties of which vegetable?

12. What is the capital city of Poland?

13. Riga is the capital city of which country?

14. Which two countries border the USA?

15. What is the term for a female fox?

16. Black Forest gateau is a type of what?

17. True or false? A croissant is a type of flower.

18. In the army, who ranks higher: a general or a major?

19. How many sides has a nonagon?

20. How many bytes in a kilobyte?

21. What is the term for the brother of your mother or father?

22. Which artist painted the inside of the Sistine Chapel?

23. Next to water, what is the most popular drink in the world?

24. In which country is the River Ganges?

25. Cirrus and cumulus are types of what?

Answers on page 76

Young Scientists in Ireland

Children in Ireland are well known for their talents in science and technology. The BT Young Scientist and Technology Exhibition will be celebrating its 50th anniversary in 2014. The event will take place in the RDS in Dublin from January 9th to 11th. If possible, why not visit on Saturday 11th? You're sure to find it very interesting. The exhibition gives teenagers a chance to show off their ideas and inventions and many participants have been very successful with their projects. Read on to find out about just a few…

Geared Up in Monaghan

Niamh Gallagher and Leanne McKenna from Saint Louis Convent in Monaghan Town participated in 2011 with their project called 'Improving Bicycle Use in Monaghan'. The girls did not win the competition. However, following the exhibition, they met with the local town council to discuss their ideas. The council rejected the idea of cycle lanes, but asked the girls to enter their other suggestions for the Department of the Environment's  'Smarter Travel' plan. They went on to secure around €140,000 for 15 bicycle shelters and 22 bicycle racks around County Monaghan. That's an amazing achievement! If you live in Monaghan (or if you ever visit), be sure to keep an eye out for those bicycle shelters and racks.

Marvellous Medical Invention

Rhona Togher, Eimear O'Carroll and Niamh Chapman from Ursuline College in Sligo participated in 2009 with their project called 'The Sound of Silence … Therapy for Tinnitus Sufferers'. (Tinnitus is a condition that causes some people to experience an uncomfortable ringing in their ears.) In addition to being the overall runner-up in the competition, the project won the Health Research

Board's special prize for medical inventions. Rhona and Eimear further developed the project and set up a company called Restored Hearing in May 2009. Since then, their company has received international interest and sales in Europe, North America and Australia. Rhona and Eimear are both studying physics at university now.

Shore to Succeed

Declan Moore, Barry Holland and David Ryan from Clonakilty Community College in Cork participated in 2012 with their project called 'Manufacture of a Nutritional Beverage … from Seaweed Extract'. The boys started making a new type of health drink in school and then brought their project to the exhibition. They called their product OceanaBoost. The drink contains extracts of bladderwrack

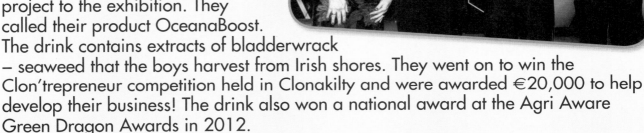

— seaweed that the boys harvest from Irish shores. They went on to win the Clon'trepreneur competition held in Clonakilty and were awarded €20,000 to help develop their business! The drink also won a national award at the Agri Aware Green Dragon Awards in 2012.

Feeling Inspired?

Here are a few ideas for science projects and competitions:

◆ **Primary Science Fair:** Primary schools can exhibit a class project at the BT Young Scientist and Technology Exhibition. There are 120 places available for 4th, 5th and 6th classes. (www.rds.ie/primarysciencefair)

◆ **Mini Scientist:** This programme is also for 4th, 5th and 6th classes. Projects are exhibited at a science fair in your school and winners are then chosen to go forward to a regional final event. (www.miniscientist.ie)

◆ **Incredible Edibles:** Ask your teacher to register for this Agri Aware project and then grow your own vegetables. (www.incredibleedibles.ie)

Aimsigh na Difríochtaí

Síleann an lucharachán go bhfuil sé greannmhar!
Aimsigh 8 ndifríocht idir na pictiúir.

Brain Teasers

1 If you were to take two apples from three apples, how many would you have?

2 If you were standing directly on Antarctica's South Pole facing north, which direction would you travel if you took one step backward?

3 Carrie Barry was born on December 21st, yet her birthday is always in the summer. How is this possible?

4 How could 'SIX KINGS' be converted into a word that describes Scandinavian seafarers of olden times?

5 Two mothers and two daughters go to a pet shop and buy three cats. Each female gets her own cat. How is this possible?

6 From what heavy seven-letter word can you take away two letters and have eight left?

7 What is half of 2 + 2?

8 How many seconds are there in a year?

9 Why is it against the law for a man living in Cork to be buried in Monaghan?

1. Two. You'd have the two that you took! **2.** North. All directions from the South Pole are north. **3.** She lives in the Southern Hemisphere. **4.** SIX = VI ← VI KINGS ← VIKINGS. **5.** There is a grandmother, a mother and a daughter. **6.** Weights. **7.** 3 (half of 2 is 1, and then 1 plus 2 is 3). **8.** 12 (January second, February second, etc!). **9.** Because he's still living!

Cone Sequence!

Look carefully at the order of the three pine cones below.
Can you find them in exactly the same order in the box?
Search from left to right, top to bottom and from the bottom upwards!

Answers on page 76

Creature Crossword

See if you can solve all these creature clues to complete the crossword.

Across

3. The second day of Christmas gift (6, 5)
4. An animal that brays (6)
8. The largest polar creature (5)
9. Santa has eight of these (8)
10. A red-breasted bird (5)

Down

1. The third day of Christmas gift (6, 4)
2. A polar animal with flippers (4)
5. A large creature with whiskers and tusks (6)
6. Grizzly and polar are types of what? (4)
7. A sea bird that lives in the South Pole (7)

What do you call a penguin in the desert?

Lost!

Answers on page 76

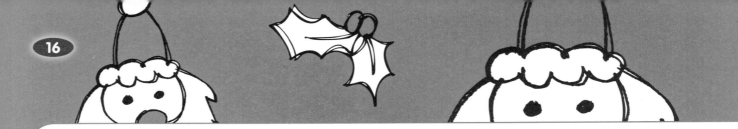

Aimsigh na Difríochtaí

Tá an crann Nollag chun titim! Aimsigh 8 ndifríocht idir na pictiúir.

Science Facts

⭐ Prairie dogs are burrowing rodents that live in the grasslands of North America. When two prairie dogs meet, they kiss to find out if they know each other! If they do not know each other, the stranger is driven away. If they do, they kiss again and then start grooming each other. How cute!

Prairie dogs

⭐ The fastest growing tree in the world is the eucalyptus. One tree in New Guinea grew a whopping 10.5 m in one year.

⭐ Around 5000 years ago, the Sahara Desert was covered with grassland and trees. Paintings found in desert caves in Algeria show giraffes, hippopotamuses, lions, and humans hunting and cattle grazing.

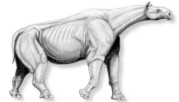

Paraceratherium

⭐ Paraceratherium is the biggest land mammal on record. It lived around 35 million years ago in Asia and Europe and was 8 m tall and 11 m long. It looked like a huge rhinoceros, but had a long neck like a giraffe. Six people, walking side by side, could easily have passed underneath it.

⭐ The sea level does not always stay the same. During the last ice age (18,000 years ago), the sea level was about 122 m lower than it is today. It was possible to walk between England and France. Since then, the sea level has risen by about 8 cm every 100 years.

⭐ The ancestors of sea mammals once lived on land. Around 50 million years ago, they began to enter the sea for food and, eventually, their bodies adapted to life in the water. The whale's front legs became flippers, its back legs disappeared and its nostrils became a blowhole on the top of its head.

⭐ Sea mammals do not have 'homes' in the water, but some have special sleeping habits. Sea otters sleep floating on the surface. They wind strands of seaweed around their bodies to stop themselves drifting. Manatees sleep near the seabed, but come to the surface every 10 minutes to breathe.

Manatee

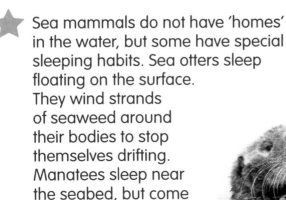

Sea otter

Pretty Poinsettias

Play this game with a friend. Choose one flower each. Take turns to roll the dice, then colour in the petal with the same number. If you've already coloured the petal, miss a turn. The first one to finish the flower is the winner.

• red	∷ orange
⁚ blue	⁙ yellow
∴ green	⸬ purple

Freaky Critters

Opossum: This is a clever marsupial from North America. It plays dead when it feels threatened and mimics the smell of a rotting corpse by producing a foul-smelling fluid. Yuck! The opossum is also immune to the venom of snakes, scorpions and bees.

Dead clever, you might say.

Pistol shrimp: Measuring only 3-5 cm long, this creature has amazing techniques for escaping danger and stunning

Pistol shrimp

I try to keep on his good side.

its prey. By snapping shut its claw, it produces a special gas-filled bubble that generates a sound of up to 218 decibels (louder than a gunshot) and allows it to travel at speeds of up to 97 km/h. When the bubble collapses, the gas inside it explodes. The explosion creates a shockwave and a light, which last for a few seconds. Surely this is the James Bond of shrimps!

Potoo: This bird lives in the rainforests of Central and South America. It eats insects and hunts by patiently sitting on a tree stump, waiting for its meals to fly by. The trick is, the potoo is an absolute master of camouflage. It also lays a single spotted egg directly on the top of a stump.

Can you spot the potoo?

Coelacanth: We've saved the best

for last! The coelacanth is a fish that grows up to 5 m long and is covered in hard, bony scales, which act as armour. It normally lives near the ocean floor. 'What's so great about that?' you might ask. This fish was thought to have become extinct at the end of the Cretaceous period, when the dinosaurs died out. This was because paleontologists found 400-million-year-old coelacanth fossils! So, not only is this a very old species, it makes you wonder what other Cretaceous creatures are hiding in the deep!

Top Trees

There are so many pretty things you can put on your Christmas tree.
Can you find them in the grid?
Look forwards, backwards, up, down and diagonally.

```
A H T S C L S T H G I L B
V Q I A L I R C G D W C E
C A N M P L H A U V D C A
X D S F W S E L D N A C L
Y N E R G F K B Z C U S O
B F L D A S T F I G T R F
S E T A L O C O H C S E R
H S P M W I B J Z E A T L
M J N Y T S Y L L O H T E
J L M O R K D B B S E I G
T P G U W I U A T D Z L N
S W O B J A A A E E Z G A
X R O M B L R F Y B V Z M
```

BOWS	GLITTER	TINSEL	SNOW
BAUBLES	ANGEL	STAR	CHOCOLATES
CANDLES	HOLLY	LIGHTS	BEADS
FAIRY	BELLS	CANDY	GIFTS

Éan Corr

Cuir ciorcal thart ar an éan corr ar gach líne.

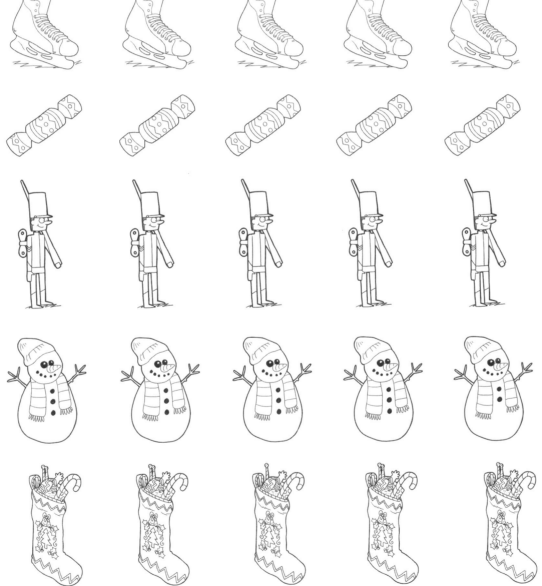

Plum Cake

What's Christmas without cake? Here's a recipe to make a mouth-watering winter plum cake!

 Here's what you will need:

- 115g (4oz) butter • 2 eggs • 1 tablespoon of baking powder
- ¼ teaspoon cinnamon • 170g (6oz) sugar • 115g (4oz) plain flour
- 1 tablespoon almond extract • 4 plums, sliced

★ Here's how to do it ★

1 Start by preheating the oven to 350°F/175°C (gas mark 4)* and greasing a 10-inch cake tin.

2 Put the butter and two-thirds of the sugar into a bowl and beat it until fluffy. Add the eggs and almond extract. Sift the flour and baking powder together and add to the mixture in the bowl. Mix together with a wooden spoon.

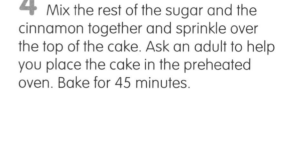

3 Pour this batter into the cake tin. Arrange the plum slices on the top of the mixture.

4 Mix the rest of the sugar and the cinnamon together and sprinkle over the top of the cake. Ask an adult to help you place the cake in the preheated oven. Bake for 45 minutes.

5 After 45 minutes, take the cake out of the oven and leave it on the worktop to cool.* Enjoy your plum cake while it's still warm!

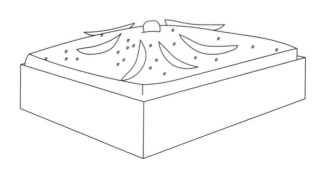

* Ask an adult to help you with this.

Chocolate Treats

Christmas just isn't Christmas without little chocolates to snack on.
So just follow this recipe and make some for you and your friends to enjoy.

Here's what you will need:

- 115g (4oz) butter • 170g (6oz) sugar • 340g (12oz) chocolate chips
- 170g (6oz) chopped walnuts • 340g (12oz) coloured mini marshmallows
- 200g (7oz) dessicated coconut •
5 sheets of waxed paper, about 23 cm (9 in) square

★ Here's how to do it ★

1 Ask an adult to help you fill ¾ of a large saucepan with hot water and place it over a low heat. Put the butter, sugar and chocolate chips in a glass mixing bowl and place it in the saucepan.

2 Stir occasionally until the butter and chocolate melt into a smooth paste. Remove from the heat and allow the mixture to cool.

3 Add the marshmallows and nuts to the chocolate mixture.

4 While the chocolate mixture is cooling, lay the sheets of wax paper on a flat surface. Sprinkle coconut on the wax paper.

5 Spoon a generous amount of the chocolate mixture on to the wax sheets. Roll up into a log shape. Leave them in the fridge overnight.

6 Take them out the next morning and cut into chunky slices. Peel off the wax paper and hey presto! A mouthwatering chocolate treat complete with a snowy winter covering!

Present Puzzle

Look at the list of exciting Christmas presents.
Find them all inside the beautifully wrapped gift box!

C	C	T	O	Y	S	P	C	O	A	O	W	C	A
O	E	W	T	T	W	P	H	W	C	W	A	A	C
M	O	M	B	E	S	A	O	S	W	C	E	M	A
P	P	E	T	S	A	S	C	W	E	L	A	E	M
U	A	R	B	H	W	H	O	R	T	O	H	R	T
T	S	B	H	O	O	A	L	O	R	T	R	A	R
E	R	O	A	E	W	L	A	T	L	H	E	S	M
R	W	O	A	S	R	E	T	S	R	E	H	A	S
S	R	K	H	W	K	H	E	O	O	S	E	R	T
E	K	S	T	A	E	M	S	E	W	H	R	H	R
W	R	I	S	T	W	A	T	C	H	E	S	H	H
E	C	W	I	T	A	W	R	W	T	W	R	S	E
W	C	A	R	D	S	A	C	T	H	W	H	R	S
R	W	E	D	L	J	E	W	E	L	L	E	R	Y

JEWELLERY   COMPUTERS

BOOKS   WRISTWATCHES

CLOTHES   CAMERAS

TOYS   PETS

CHOCOLATES   CARDS

SHOES

Snowy Crossword

Solve these snowy clues and write in the words to complete the crossword. We've filled in one answer to get you started.

Across
1. A domed house made of snow (5)
3. Frozen rain (4)
5. A major snowstorm (8)
7. A hanging frozen spike (6)
8. Jack's icy coating (5)
10. Tiny ice formation with six points (9)

Down
2. Slow-moving ice mass (7)
4. Fast-moving mass of falling snow (9)
6. Snow piled up by the wind (5)
9. Areas of snow and ice covering the Earth's poles (4)

What do you get if you cross a snowman with a shark?

Frostbite!

Answers on page 77

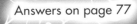

Fun Snowflakes

How about adding some snowflake decorations to your home? Follow these simple instructions and have fun making unique, dazzling snowflakes!

 Here's what you will need:

l Sheet of white paper l Pencil l Stapler l Scissors l Thread l Glue

Here's how to do it

1 Along the short edge, concertina fold the paper six to eight times. Fold lightly in half and mark the centre with a pencil.

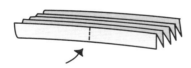

2 Cut the ends of the concertina into points. Cut triangular shapes out of the sides, taking care not to cut away all of the folded edge. Staple the centre together (see diagram).

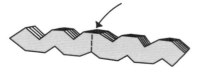

3 Open out the concertina and glue the ends together.

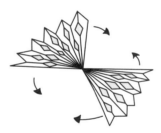

4 Knot a length of thread to the snowflake so that you can hang it up. Hang your snowflake on the Christmas tree or use it as a window decoration!

Aimsigh na Difríochtaí

Is breá leis an bhfear seo dinnéar na Nollag a chócaráil!
Aimsigh 8 ndifríocht idir na pictiúir.

Quiz Master

1. Which artist famously painted sunflowers?

2. In which town do the Flintstones live?

3. What is the name of Harry Potter's pet owl?

4. Who were the rulers of Ancient Egypt?

5. Which author created the character Tracy Beaker?

6. Cocker, Springer and King Charles are varieties of which breed of dog?

7. The fighters who competed in Ancient Rome were called what?

8. What is the largest planet in the Solar System?

9. True or false? A hyacinth is a type of fish.

10. The cob and pen are the male and female of which aquatic bird?

11. In which county in Ireland are the Cliffs of Moher located?

12. Which country has won the FIFA World Cup the most?

13. What is the capital city of Australia?

14. In what country is the Stromboli volcano located?

15. Caracas is the capital city of which country?

16. What is the line of latitude that runs around the middle of the Earth called?

17. Which car maker makes the Fiesta, Ka and Mondeo?

18. Pavlova and banoffie are types of what?

19. True or false? A catamaran is a type of boat.

20. True or false? A skink is a type of snake.

21. What is 7^2?

22. Which company makes the Xbox?

23. Where would you find the Sea of Tranquility?

24. Who directed the *Lord of the Rings* trilogy?

25. What is the term for a structure built by the Ancient Romans to carry water?

Answers on page 77

The Tale of Good King Wenceslas

Have you ever heard the Christmas carol 'Good King Wenceslas' and wondered who it is about? Wenceslas was born in Prague in 907 AD, in the territory that was then known as Bohemia, and is now the Czech Republic. He was the Duke of Bohemia from 925 to 935 and his family life is a dark tale of betrayal and murder. This is his story.

In the ninth century, Bohemia was a pagan country with wild, barbarian tribes. Borivoi and Ludmilla were the Duke and Duchess of Bohemia. In 871, they decided to convert to Christianity. So too did the members of their court in Prague. However, most of the people in the country continued with their pagan practices and they ran Borivoi and Ludmilla out of the country. Eventually, they returned and had a son called Wratislaw. When he grew up, he married a noble woman named Drahomira. Wenceslas was their first child. Over the years, they had five more children: four daughters and a second son called Boleslav.

The Duchess Ludmilla hoped that her grandson, Wenceslas, would grow up to be a good Christian ruler, but she did not like Drahomira and was suspicious of her true intentions. She was becoming very powerful among the nobles of the country and it was clear that she had ambitions of her own. Ludmilla decided to take charge of the boy's education. He studied the bible and learned Latin and Greek. Ludmilla also made sure that he helped with the annual harvest at her castle in Tetin.

In 921, when Wenceslas was 13, his father Wratislaw was killed in battle. Because he was too young to rule, it was decided that his mother would reign in his place. It turned out that Ludmilla was right to be suspicious of Drahomira. She wanted all of Bohemia to return to pagan practices and immediately began to persecute Christians and order the killing of priests.

Ludmilla escaped from the court and fled to her castle in Tetin, where she hoped to live out her days in peace. But Drahomira had other plans. She was jealous of Ludmilla's influence over her son and sent two of her nobles to Tetin to assassinate her. Ludmilla received the nobles in her home as guests and they strangled her with her veil.

Wenceslas was forced to take part in pagan ceremonies or else risk being murdered like his grandmother, but secretly he continued in his own beliefs. When he was 18, the remaining Christian nobles supported him in a rebellion against his mother. The uprising was successful and Drahomira was sent into exile for her wickedness. Wenceslas became the Duke of Bohemia and promised to rule with justice and mercy. He ended persecution and provided housing and clothing for the poor. It was said that he brought them food and firewood himself in the middle of the night, so they would not be embarrassed by having others know how destitute they were. He pardoned many prisoners and released them from jail. He also pardoned his mother and allowed her to return from exile. The people loved him for his kindness.

However, many of the nobles were unhappy with Wenceslas. They said he was soft and too religious. They wanted Bohemia to go to war in order to gain independence from the German Empire, but Wenceslas was against bloodshed. They began secretly to plot against him. And who do you think was their leader? That's right: his mother Drahomira. She convinced Boleslav, her younger son, to join her by reminding him that he would become the Duke of Bohemia if they got rid of his brother.

In 935, Wenceslas visited the city where Boleslav lived. An important religious feast was taking place. He accepted an invitation from his brother to stay the night at his castle. Boleslav's wife Biagota was due to have a baby, so it was a time of celebration. The brothers passed an enjoyable evening together and the following morning, Wenceslas left the castle and went to church.

Wenceslas was surprised to meet Boleslav on the church steps – after all he had just left the castle. He greeted him warmly and thanked him for his hospitality. Boleslav replied: "Yesterday I did my best to serve you fittingly, but this must be my service today…" With that, he drew his sword and lunged at Wenceslas. A struggle began and a number of nobles joined in to support Boleslav. Wenceslas was outnumbered and was fatally stabbed. As he lay dying at the church door, his last words were, "May God forgive you for this deed, my brother." It was said that Boleslav's baby son was born at precisely the moment Wenceslas died. He was named Strachkvas, which means 'terrible feast'. Boleslav became the Duke of Bohemia. In history, he is known as Boleslav the Cruel. Wenceslas is the patron saint of the Czech Republic.

Sweetie Jumble

These sweets are ready to be put into one giant bag of Christmas treats!
Unjumble the letters to find out the flavour of each sweet.

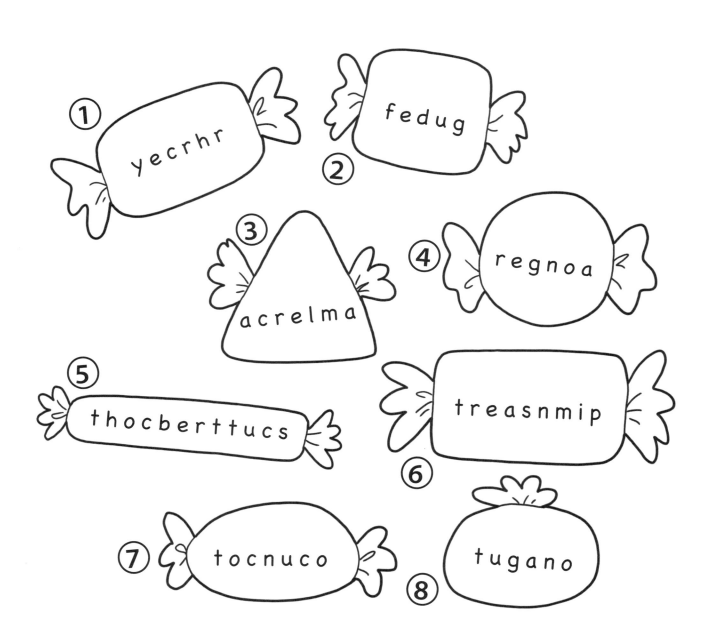

1. yecrhr
2. fedug
3. acrelma
4. regnoa
5. thocberttucs
6. treasnmip
7. tocnuco
8. tugano

Answers on page 77

Food Fooler

There are lots of extra-scrummy things to eat and drink during the festive season! See if you can think of a food or drink beginning with each letter in the word 'Christmas'.

C ....

H ....

R ....

I ....

S ....

T ....

M...

A ....

S ....

Aimsigh na Difríochtaí

Bí ag faire amach don fhear sneachta! Aimsigh 8 ndifríocht idir na pictiúir.

Matching Cards

At first glance it seems that two people have sent you the same Christmas card! But look closer – can you spot five differences between the two designs?

Colourful Candles

Colour in this festive candleholder. Then draw and decorate your own glowing Christmas candles!

How long does it take a Christmas candle to burn down?

About a wick!

36 # Get Down

Jack is about to tackle the toughest trail on the slopes. Can you help him find his way safely to the bottom of the mountain? Just one trail will take him there.

When you're done, write the letters you found along the route in order in the spaces below to see the answer to the riddle.

Answer on page 77

Start

Why don't mountains get cold in the winter?

_____ _____ _____ _____ _____ _____ _____

Illustrated by Steve Skelton

Picture Puzzler

Illustrated by Erin Mauterer

What's Wrong?™

How many silly things can you find in this picture?

Picture Puzzler

Illustrated by Michael Palan

Use the first letter of each word pictured below to spell school-related words.

For example, the top word across is STUDY:

sun   trophy   umbrella   drum   yarn

Words go across and down.

How many can you figure out?

Picture Puzzler

Illustrated by James Yamasaki

Find the path through Chillville from Start to Finish. (Watch out for one-way streets!)

BONUS
Find at least two
- chilly children
- chilled things
- chili dogs
- things that rhyme with chill

Maze answer on page 77

Picture Puzzler

Illustrated by Mary Sullivan

See if you can find:
- the lost bike shown on the poster
- two maps, two bows, two purses, two newspapers and two masks
- two creatures and two items that appear twice in the scene
- the following hidden objects: teacup, candle, muffin, slice of cake, spoon, chili pepper, umbrella, plunger, ring, slice of pizza, shoe, clothes hanger

Hidden Pictures™
Aimsigh Iad

An féidir leat teacht ar na rudaí seo atá i bhfolach sa phictiúr?

Freagraí ar leathanach 77

Illustrated by Dave Klug

snáth

bior

stoca

maighnéad

clog

bróg

iasc

scuab fiacla

gé

crián

cairéad

miotóg

tóirse

iarann

peann luaidhe

cleite

club gailf

peann

scaif

crios

cupán

scuab péinteála

casúr

banana

ráca

bád

Aimsigh na Difríochtaí

An féidir leat teacht ar **20** difríocht, ar a laghad, idir na pictiúir?

Freagraí ar leathanach 78

RENTALS

Illustrated by Tim Haggerty

Ní fíor-chalóg shneachta ceann amháin de na calóga thíos. Cé acu?

Time to Rhyme

Grab a pencil; away you go.
It's time to use the rhymes you know.
Every clue has a rhyming hint,
About the word you need to print.
To start things off, we filled in one.
Now try the rest and have some fun!

Answers on page 78

Across

1. Baseball stick; rhymes with **cat**
3. Banana or apple; rhymes with **toot**
6. Opposite of yes; rhymes with **row**
7. A pronoun for a thing; rhymes with **pit**
9. A brief sleep; rhymes with **map**
12. Small child; rhymes with **lot**
14. Unit of weight; rhymes with **jam**
16. To cry hard; rhymes with **cob**
18. Worn around the neck; rhymes with **fly**
19. Icy flakes; rhymes with **grow**
21. Steal; rhymes with **job**
24. A part of the body; rhymes with **hear**
25. A pronoun like us; rhymes with **flea**
26. Opposite of stop; rhymes with **low**
29. A colour name; rhymes with **queen**
30. A female chicken; rhymes with **ten**

Down

1. Use this to catch fish; rhymes with **skate**
2. Opposite of from; rhymes with **zoo**
3. A snake's tooth; rhymes with **bang**
4. Opposite of out; rhymes with **win**
5. A part of your foot; rhymes with **doe**
8. Throw a ball; rhymes with **gloss**
10. A type of museum; rhymes with **dart**
11. Two of a kind; rhymes with **hair**
13. A musical pitch; rhymes with **cone**
15. A cat sound; rhymes with **sea cow**
17. A type of snake; rhymes with **Noah**
20. A small bird; rhymes with **ten**
22. A vegetable; rhymes with **mean**
23. A breakfast food; rhymes with **leg**
27. Either ___; rhymes with **score**
28. An exclamation; rhymes with **no**

Art Qs

Answers on page 78

Art Smart

Can you find five differences between these two pieces of art?

Who's Who?

Some of these people were famous painters. Do you know which ones?

Charles Dickens

Pablo Picasso

Leonardo DaVinci

Ty Cobb

Claude Monet

Isaac Newton

Amelia Earhart

Georgia O'Keeffe

Mall Wall

You've been hired to paint a mural on a mall's wall. What will your mural look like? Draw it here.

How Mod!

When you look at a piece of modern art, you might see many different shapes and colours. When you look at the words 'modern art', you might see lots of different words. Can you make at least 15 words from the letters in MODERN ART?

_____
_____
_____
_____
_____
_____
_____
_____
_____
_____
_____
_____
_____
_____
_____
_____
_____

Museum Maze

Help Art catch up to his class at the museum.

Start

Finish

JumBled Art

Unscramble each set of letters to get the name of an art supply.

NAPIT   _ _ _ _ _

SEALE   _ _ _ _ _

SHRUB   _ _ _ _ _

PREAP   _ _ _ _ _

ARKREM   _ _ _ _ _ _

VASCAN   _ _ _ _ _ _

Puzzles by Lori Mortensen   Illustrated by Mike Moran

Penguin Path

This penguin is hungry! Can you help him slip and slide down a path that leads into the water so he can fish for food? Be careful not to crash into any other penguins.

Answer on page 79

Start

Finish

Illustrated by Dan McGeehan

Highlights

The Hole Story

What a find! Doug just dug up something completely unexpected. What do you think he discovered? Draw it here.

Deireadh

Picture Puzzler

Illustrated by Chuck Dillon

Highlights

What's Wrong?™
How many silly things can you find in this picture?

Dog Days

Anna, Sophie, Rex and Spencer each entered a dog in the Dapper Dog Show. Each dog won an award. Can you match each person with his or her dog and the dog's award?

Use the chart to keep track of your answers. Put an **X** in each box that can't be true and an **O** in boxes that match.

Answers on page 79

	Anna	Sophie	Rex	Spencer
Springer Spaniel				
Mixed Breed				
Jack Russell				
Basset Hound				
Best Bark				
Best Trick				
Friendliest				
Best in Show				

1. Spencer's dog won the Friendliest award.
2. Rex's dog took Best Trick, but the Jack Russell did not.
3. The Springer spaniel, who shares the same first initial as its owner, won Best Bark.
4. The basset hound won Best in Show.

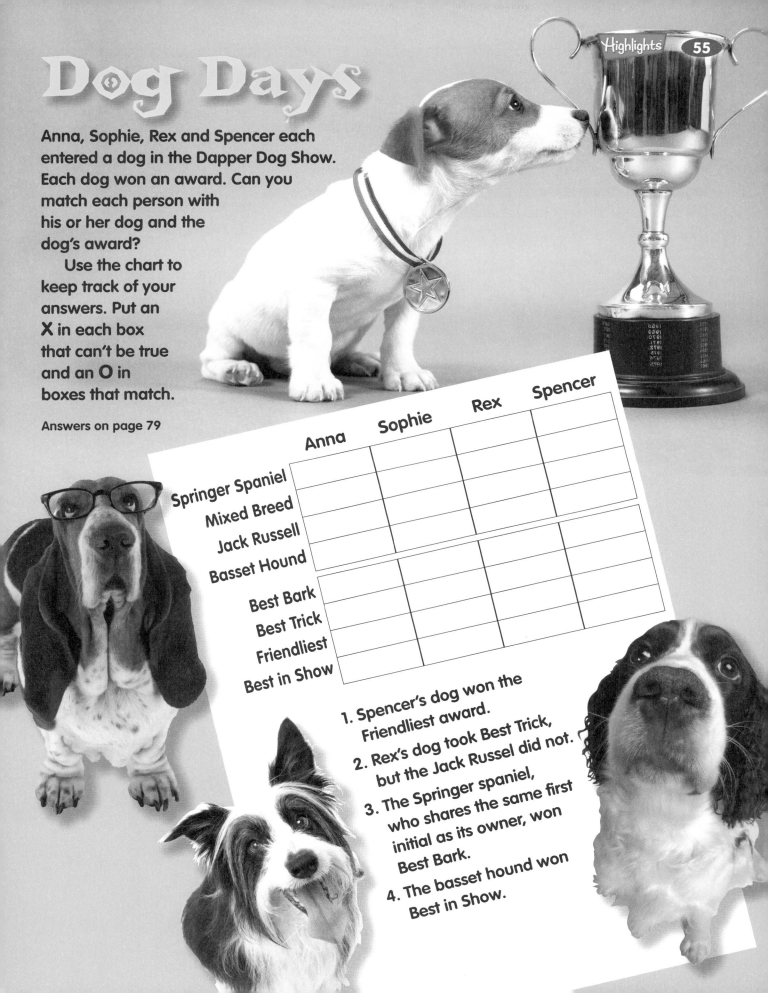

HiLARiOUS!

These hyenas have a serious case of the ha-has. They must be laughing at the funny words hidden in the grid on the next page. See how many you can find by looking up, down, across, backwards and diagonally. Be careful—many of the letters appear in more than one word.

Answers on page 79

WORD LIST

~~ABSURD~~	JEST
AMUSE	JOKE
BIT	JOLLY
CACKLE	JOY
CHUCKLE	LAUGH
CLOWN	MIRTH
COMEDY	PRANK
FARCE	PUN
FROLIC	QUIP
FUN	RIDDLE
GAG	SKIT
GIGGLE	SMILE
GLEE	SMIRK
GRIN	STUNT
GUFFAW	TEE HEE
HA HA	TICKLE
HAPPY	ZANY
HILARITY	

Rain Forest Qs

Answers on page 79

Jungle Journey

This scientist has gotten lost in the rain forest. Can you help her find the way back to her canoe?

Start

Finish

Illustrated by Mike Moran   Puzzles by Carly Schuna

Twin Toucans

Which two toucan pictures are exactly alike?

A

B

C

D

Rain Forest Quiz Match each question to the right answer.

1. Continent with the most rain forest land   a. Okapi

2. World's largest rain forest river   b. Africa

3. Zebra-like rain forest animal   c. Blue Morpho

4. Rain forest butterfly   d. Amazon

5. Continent that's home to the Congo Rain Forest   e. South America

Creature or Not?

Some of these are rain forest creatures and some are imposters. Can you tell which are the real critters?

CHIMICHANGA or CHIMPANZEE?

GIBBON or RIBBON?

FEMUR or LEMUR?

PIRANHA or KIELBASA?

ANACONDA or EMPANADA?

STAMEN or CAIMAN?

M ss ng V w ls

NMLS is the word 'animals' with the vowels taken away. Can you identify each of these tropical rain forest animals?

SPDR MNKY

TR FRG

GRLL

JGR

RNGTN

New Species

More than half of the world's plant and animal species live in the rain forest. Scientists estimate that millions of rain forest species are still undiscovered. What new living thing would you like to find? Draw it here.

Picture Puzzler

Illustrated by Helena Bogosian

Which candy was not used on the gingerbread house?
Which candy was used but isn't shown here?

Answers on page 80

Raise the Flag

Fiona is forming her own country! Now she needs a flag.
What do you think her country's flag should look like?
Design it here.

Monkey Business

It's time to monkey around! Each of these primate names fits into the grid in just one way. Use the size of each word as a clue to where it might fit. When you're done, write the letters from the shaded squares in order in the spaces below to see the answer to the riddle.

Answers on page 80

Word List

3 letters
APE

4 letters
~~DOUC~~

5 letters
LEMUR
LORIS
POTTO

6 letters
AYE-AYE
BABOON
BONOBO
GALAGO
GIBBON
LANGUR
MONKEY

7 letters
COLOBUS
GORILLA
MACAQUE
TAMARIN
TARSIER

8 letters
MANDRILL
MARMOSET

9 letters
ORANGUTAN

10 letters
CHIMPANZEE

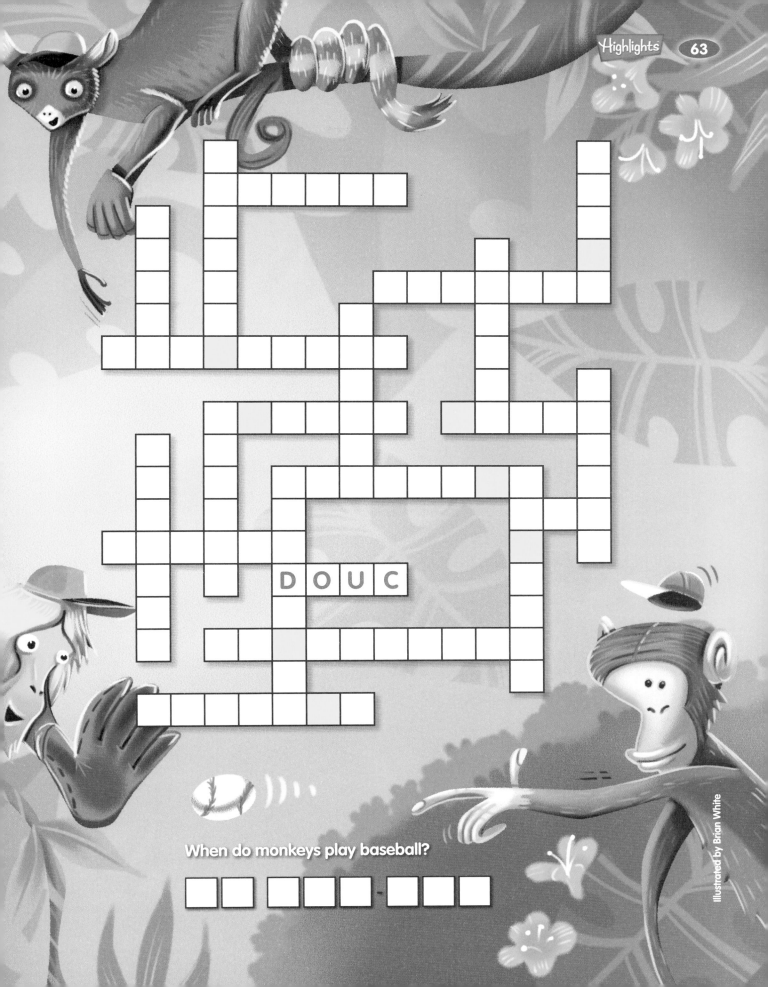

D O U C

When do monkeys play baseball?

Picture Puzzler

There are at least 8 differences between these two scenes.

How many can you find?

Super Challenge: Find 20 differences!

Be Seated

Mr. Ease has six boys and six girls in his class: Aiden, Brian, Carlos, Dave, Eric and Frank; Grace, Haley, Iris, Jada, Katie and Lily. But who sits where? Use the clues below to figure out which seat belongs to which kid. The numbers on the chairs will help.

Answers on page 80

1. Dave sits in the seat farthest from the clock.
2. Brian sits between Lily and Katie and behind Haley.
3. Eric sits between Haley and Jada, behind Iris and in front of Lily.
4. The girls all sit in even-numbered seats, the boys in odd-numbered seats.
5. Grace, Carlos and Katie sit in the rows farthest away from the windows.
6. Jada sits behind Frank and in front of Dave.

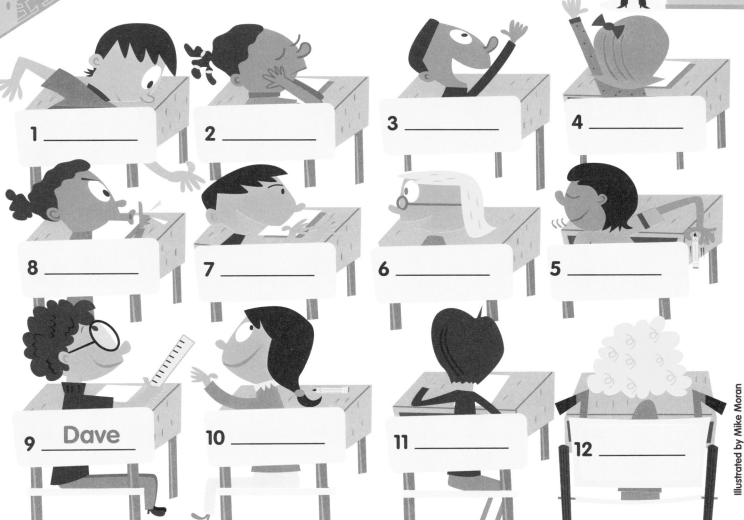

1 _____   2 _____   3 _____   4 _____

8 _____   7 _____   6 _____   5 _____

9 Dave   10 _____   11 _____   12 _____

Illustrated by Mike Moran

Cad atá Cearr?

An féidir leat teacht ar 25 rud amaideacha nó níos mó, atá ag tarlú sa phictiúr seo?

Illustrated by Dave Clegg

Reptile Qs

Later, 'Gator

This alligator wants to soak up some sun. Can you help him reach his favourite spot?

Start

Finish

Reptile Report

Some of these reptile facts are true and some are false. Can you tell which are true?

a. All reptiles are cold-blooded.

T or F

b. All reptiles lay eggs.

T or F

c. The Komodo dragon is the smallest species of lizard.

T or F

d. Snakes are able to smell with their tongues.

T or F

Reptile or Amphibian?

Some of these are reptiles and some are amphibians. Can you pick out the reptiles?

LIZARD or SALAMANDER?

NEWT or IGUANA?

TREE FROG or SEA TURTLE?

SKINK or TOAD?

PYTHON or MUDPUPPY?

Puzzles by Carly Schuna   Illustrated by Mike Moran

M ss ng V w ls

RPTLS is the word 'reptiles' with the vowels taken away. Can you figure out the names of these five RPTLS?

_____

RTTLSNK

_____

CRCDL

_____

VPR

_____

GCK

_____

CHMLN

Look-Alike Lizards

Which two chameleons are exactly the same?

Turtle Doodle

Some species of turtles have detailed patterns on their shells. Draw your own pattern here.

Answers on page 80

Picture Puzzler

Can you find at least 10 differences between these two photos?

Map Mix-Up

People are flocking to Logicville for the big Summer Festival. Unfortunately, the new town maps were printed without labels on most of the buildings on Main Street. To help the lost tourists, read the clues below to figure out which building is which. Fill in the correct names on the map.

1. Archie's Arcade is one building south of the Sandwich Hut.
2. Izzy's Ice Cream is northeast of Archie's Arcade.
3. The Movie Palace is north of Sim's Sweets.
4. The T-Shirt Shack is one building south of Izzy's.

Answers on page 80

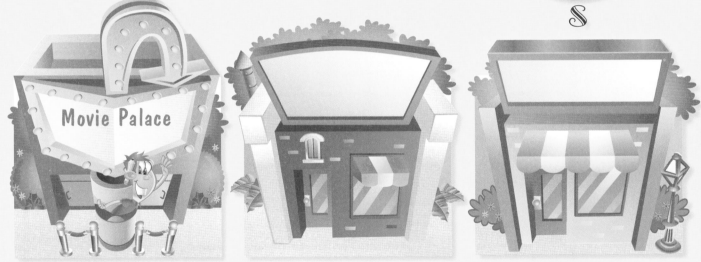

Puzzle by Sara Matson

Illustrated by Garry Colby

Ready, Set, Grow!

This community garden is growing in popularity. Can you help Rosemary meet her friend Tom so they can water their plants? Just one path will take her there.

Answers on page 80

Start

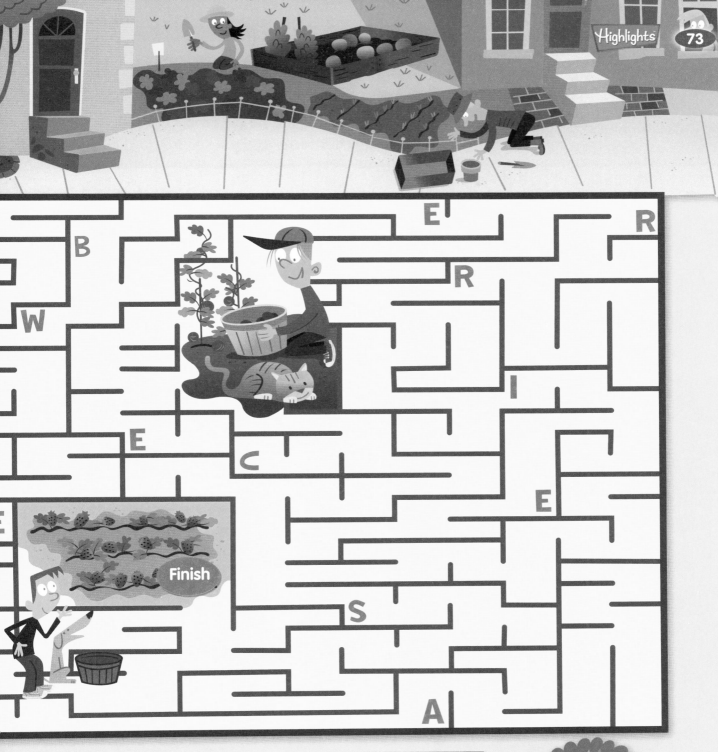

The maze contains the letters: E, R, B, R, W, I, E, C, E, S, A

Bonus Puzzle

Once you've found the correct path, write the letters along it in order in the spaces below. They'll answer this riddle:

What is a scarecrow's favourite fruit?

__ __ __ __ __ __ __ __ __ __ __

Illustrated by Jim Paillot

Cad atá Cearr?

An féidir leat teacht ar 25 rud amaideacha nó níos mó, atá ag tarlú sa phictiúr seo?

Illustrated by Tim Haggerty

Page 4:

Across: 2. Usher, **3.** Beyonce, **4.** Pink, **6.** Daft Punk, **7.** Pitbull, **8.** Lady Gaga, **13.** One Direction, **15.** Bruno Mars, **17.** Demi Lovato, **18.** Will.I.Am, **19.** Nicki Minaj

Down: 1. Justin Timberlake, **5.** Taylor Swift, **9.** Jessie J, **10.** Selena Gomez, **11.** Akon, **12.** Cody Simpson, **14.** Rihanna, **16.** Baauer, **20.** Adele

Page 6:

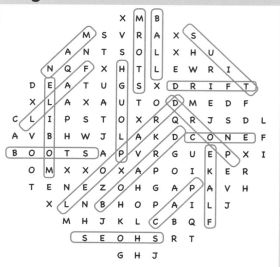

Page 8:

Page 9:

1. Robin Hood. **2.** Merlin. **3.** Florence Nightingale. **4.** Table tennis. **5.** Egypt. **6.** Aslan. **7.** Denmark. **8.** The *Titanic*. **9.** X-Men. **10.** Swimming. **11.** Potato. **12.** Warsaw. **13.** Latvia. **14.** Mexico and Canada. **15.** Vixen. **16.** Cake. **17.** False (type of pastry). **18.** General. **19.** Nine. **20.** 1000. **21.** Uncle. **22.** Michelangelo. **23.** Tea. **24.** India. **25.** Cloud.

Page 14:

Page 15:

Across: 3. Turtle doves, **4.** Donkey, **8.** whale, **9.** Reindeer, **10.** Robin
Down: 1. French hens, **2.** Seal, **5.** Walrus, **6.** Bear, **7.** Penguin

Page 20:

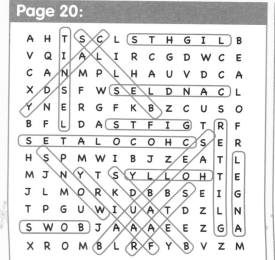

Page 24:

Page 25:

Across: 1. Igloo, 3. Hail, 5. Blizzard, 7. Icicle, 8. Frost, 10. Snowflake
Down: 2. Glacier, 4. Avalanche, 6. Drift, 9. Caps

Page 32:

1. Cherry.
2. Fudge.
3. Caramel.
4. Orange.
5. Butterscotch.
6. Spearmint.
7. Coconut.
8. Nougat.

Page 39:

words across:
STUDY, ART, GRADES, LIBRARY, KNOW, MATH, EDUCATION, PAPER, SKILL, CLASS, PENCIL, HALL, TUTOR, NOTEBOOK, HOMEWORK.

words down:
ATLAS, PLAYGROUND, BACKPACK, TEST, TEACHER, APPLE, GYM, POEM, TEAM, READ, COMPUTER, DESK, BOOK, LESSON, SPORT, LUNCH.

Page 28:

1. Vincent Van Gogh. 2. Bedrock.
3. Hedwig. 4. Pharaohs.
5. Jacqueline Wilson. 6. Spaniel.
7. Gladiators. 8. Jupiter.
9. False (type of flower). 10. Swan.
11. Clare. 12. Brazil. 13. Canberra.
14. Italy. 15. Venezuela. 16. Equator.
17. Ford. 18. Dessert. 19. True.
20. False (type of lizard).
21. 49. 22. Microsoft.
23. On the moon. 24. Peter Jackson.
25. Aqueduct.

Pages 36–37:

Why don't mountains get cold in the winter?
THEY WEAR SNOW CAPS.

Pages 42–43:

Page 40:

Page 41:

Answers

Pages 44–45:

The star is not a real snowflake. All snowflakes have six points.

Pages 46–47:

Pages 48–49:

Art Smart

How Mod!
Here are some words we found.
You may have found others.

arm	nod	tame
donate	note	tar
ear	oar	team
errand	rare	toad
moan	read	trend

Museum Maze

Who's Who?
The painters are:
Picasso
DaVinci
Monet
O'Keeffe

Jumbled Art
paint
easel
brush
paper
marker
canvas

Answers

Page 50:

Pages 52–53:

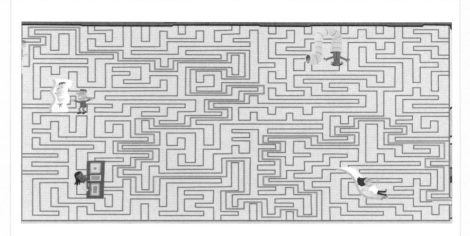

Page 55:

Anna:
Basset Hound
Best in Show

Sophie:
Springer Spaniel
Best Bark

Rex:
Mixed Breed
Best Trick

Spencer:
Jack Russell
Friendliest

Pages 56–57:

Pages 58–59:

Jungle Journey

Twin Toucans

Rain Forest Quiz
1. e
2. d
3. a
4. c
5. b

Creature or Not?
chimpanzee
gibbon
lemur
piranha
anaconda
caiman

Missing Vowels
spider monkey
tree frog
gorilla
jaguar
orangutan

Page 60:

The ___ was not used on the gingerbread house.

The ___ was.

Pages 68–69:

Later, 'Gator

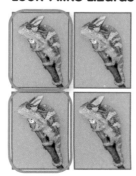

Reptile Report

a. All reptiles are cold-blooded. T
b. All reptiles lay eggs. F
c. The Komodo dragon is the smallest species of lizard. F
d. Snakes are able to smell with their tongues. T

Reptile or Amphibian?

LIZARD, IGUANA, SEA TURTLE
SKINK, PYTHON

Missing Vowels

RATTLESNAKE, CROCODILE
VIPER, GECKO, CHAMELEON

Look-Alike Lizards

Pages 62–63:

When do monkeys play baseball? IN APE-RIL

Page 65:

1. Frank
2. Iris
3. Aiden
4. Grace
5. Carlos
6. Haley
7. Eric
8. Jada
9. Dave
10. Lily
11. Brian
12. Katie

Page 71:

Movie Palace—Sandwich Hut—Izzy's Ice Cream
Sim's Sweets—Archie's Arcade—T-Shirt Shack

Pages 72–73:

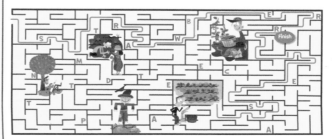

What is a scarecrow's favourite fruit? STRAWBERRIES